Chronicles of Faith

CHRONICLES OF FAITH

A CATHOLIC PERSPECTIVE ON C.S. LEWIS

BISHOP FINTAN MONAHAN

Our Sunday Visitor
Huntington, Indiana

Originally published by Veritas Publications, www.veritas.ie
This edition published by Our Sunday Visitor, Inc., in 2024

29 28 27 26 25 24 1 2 3 4 5 6 7 8 9

Our Sunday Visitor Publishing Division
Our Sunday Visitor, Inc.
200 Noll Plaza
Huntington, IN 46750
1-800-348-2440

ISBN: 978-1-63966-160-2 (Inventory No. T2866)
eISBN: 978-1-63966-161-9
LCCN: 2024930261

Cover design: Tyler Ottinger
Cover art: Original painting of C. S. Lewis by Harry Guinane
Interior design: Amanda Falk

Printed in the United States of America

Contents

God cannot give us a happiness and peace apart from himself, because it is not there. There is no such thing.

C. S. LEWIS, *Mere Christianity*

Foreword

As a young American student, I came down with a terrible disease called Anglophilia — the love of all things English. This infection first got established by a boyhood love of books. It grew worse after a visit to England and moved into a terminal condition by an excessive intake of English literature at college — especially by the writers T. S. Eliot, J. R. R. Tolkien, and C. S. Lewis.

The illness was exacerbated when a friend gave me a book called *C. S. Lewis: Images of His World.* This book was filled with photographs of the creamy limestone towers of Oxford and dreamy, mist-drenched hills of England. There were images of tweed-clad dons puffing pipes in cozy common rooms and students studying in venerable book-lined libraries or cycling off to lectures with academic gowns fluttering. I was enchanted. I wanted to live in England, and when I was offered a place to study theology at Oxford, I jumped at the chance.

Central to this dream of an English idyll was a man who was my English idol: C. S. Lewis. What was the magical spell that the creator of Aslan and Screwtape cast over an American youth who had been brought up in a fundamentalist, evangelical home? With his brilliant academic credentials and sharp argumentation, he provided a way to be a Christian and also be smart. His writings defending and explaining the Christian faith were a cool, refreshing shower washing away the grime of harsh, hot, Gospel fundamentalism. His uncompromising defense of Christian doctrine and morality cut through the sentimentalism and self-absorbed idiocy of modernistic theologians and churchmen. As I pursued the path of becoming a priest in the Church of England, Lewis was an energizing tonic, a creative inspiration, and a reassuring mentor.

The influence Lewis had on my younger self can be multiplied literally by the millions, and his influence continues to spiral upward. Biographers have studied his life, filmmakers have made his children's books come alive, and his thought has sparked debate, answered questions, and brought many a reader into a fresh experience of the Christian faith. Along with his friend Tolkien, Lewis will undoubtedly rank as one of the twentieth century's most influential writers and one of the most effective apologists in the modern age.

But Lewis was an Anglican — a Protestant! Why should Catholics be interested? Bishop Fintan Monahan has written an excellent introduction to Lewis and his work. Drawing from various biographies of Lewis as well as Lewis's own writings, Bishop Monahan walks us through Lewis's remarkable life, introducing us to the man's joys and sorrows and helping us to understand the pressures and pleasures that helped form the man and his writing.

A friend of Lewis's once commented that Lewis was "the most thoroughly converted man" he had ever met. And this is the secret of C. S. Lewis — a secret that inspires both Protestants and Catholics: Lewis was so deeply and thoroughly converted from atheism that he become a faithful disciple of the Lord Jesus Christ. Lewis's humility and down-to-earth writing style radiate through both his nonfiction philosophical and theological writing as well as his fiction and fantasy books. Although he was a top-ranking English academic, he wrote for the Everyman — and this accessible and attractive style is the secret to his success.

Lewis, an Irish Protestant, was deeply sympathetic and appreciative of his Catholic friends, and over the years countless Catholics have been delighted and educated by his writings. This is because Lewis wrote about "mere Christianity." He gets Christians of all traditions back to the basics. I have explained in my own works how Catholicism is "more Christianity" and not just "mere Christianity," but that is not to knock Lewis's thought — simply to add to it. While Catholics may not find the "fullness of the faith" in his works, because he writes about the basics, one will rarely find anything that contradicts the Catholic Faith. Lewis provides the bread. Catholicism adds the butter and jam.

Indeed, in this age when so many Catholics are poorly catechized and falling away from the historic faith, I believe Lewis the Protestant writer is "more Catholic" than many Catholics.

Bishop Monahan's book will introduce many readers not only to the fascinating life of Lewis, but will also open the wardrobe door to the world of Lewis — a world that is now over a century old, yet a world that is abundant with fresh thought, vibrant philosophy, and vividly creative alternative realms that are full of marvels and miracles, and are imbued with the radiance of a real and radical Christian faith.

Fr. Dwight Longenecker

Introduction

In previous books of this series, Bishop Fintan has examined the lives of two towering figures, John Henry Newman and Thomas Merton. Newman was an English Anglican priest, theologian, scholar, and poet, and latter Cardinal Newman. Thomas Merton, OCSO, was an American Trappist monk, writer, theologian, mystic, poet, and scholar of comparative religion. Both Newman and Merton were beloved, respected, and oft quoted by Catholics and Anglicans alike. Now, in this latest biography, Bishop Fintan explores the life and work of C. S. Lewis, popular theologian, scholar, poet, novelist, and dramatist. I only hesitate to call him avowedly Anglican because, while much of his devotional life took place within the context of the Anglican Church, Lewis was not overly factional by temperament or conviction. Perhaps his unresolved cultural identity, born and initially raised in Belfast yet largely educated in England, and belonging wholly in neither milieu, may similarly have contributed to a certain denominational ambivalence.

Nevertheless, in the introduction Bishop Fintan raises important — vitally important — questions about ecumenism and particularly the relationship between Catholicism and Anglicanism. To an Anglican there is no such thing as the Catholic faith any more than there is the Anglican faith; instead, we both share and are components, of varying sizes, of the Christian faith. There are individual churches, denominations, and traditions to be sure, but they all partake in, and are constituent parts of, the larger and unified church of all Christians that exists as yet only in potential. Most importantly, we share the same faith.

We might therefore be rather bemused about the notion of Lewis taking the "final step" to become a Catholic, for Anglicanism is the church for us — not an ecclesial community, but the church, our church, as complete and as incomplete as any other, sharing in the wounds of fracture, division, and provisionality that mark and impair all churches alike.

In *Mere Christianity*, Lewis begins with a description of Christianity as a big house with many rooms representing the many church denominations — and in this Lewis is very Anglican. Personally, I employ the analogy of a pie, with one traditional view holding that the Catholic Church is the whole pie, the whole and complete church, and that other denominations are perhaps parts of the crust that have crumbled onto the table. I, as an Anglican, however, would argue that the Catholic Church is indeed an exceedingly large slice, but that other churches are also slices of that same pie, sometimes perhaps on different plates, in the past and at our worst on different tables, but that together we could represent something so much greater than the sum of our parts; a Christian family healed, reunited, remade, but in a new form, subsuming but different from everything that currently exists. Seen in this way, ecumenism becomes a much greater vision than simply you-come-in-ism.

Turning from the important questions and challenges that Bishop Fintan credibly poses in the Introduction, I now move to a key insight that he offers toward the end of this work, as he takes stock of the different phases and influences of Lewis's life, the joy and the sorrow, and the place to where this pilgrimage of faith has brought him. Lewis's trilemma, for example, while much cited, provides a snapshot of his theology at a certain time and at a certain stage of his life, where he is more forthright and unequivocal. Philosophically, logically, rather simplistic, and unattractively emphatic, the syllogism makes no room for the insights of modern biblical scholarship which might question whether all the claims about Jesus were made solely by Jesus himself, or partly by others.

Bishop Fintan then poses the intriguing question whether *Surprised by Joy*, through his unexpected and initially "technical" marriage to Joy Davidman and the subsequent blossoming of their love for one another, Lewis's theology became later tempered, humanized, more measured. Partly through the elating, life-giving but unsettling experience of simply loving another, but also through the bewildering devastation of her untimely loss to cancer, mirroring the tragic loss of his own mother at a tender age. The boy and young man, in reaction to such pain, had once rejected the Christian faith, but then came to a later devout, albeit at times rigid, conviction. In *A Grief Observed*, Lewis wrote of knowing despair, doubt, uncertainty, emptiness, to some extent resolved as he worked through his bereavement and the writing of the book, but which left their mark upon the man, with a theology of arguably greater gradation and nuance.

Fintan, bishop and experienced pastor, ultimately reminds us that Lewis, the man, the Christian — indeed any human being — must be seen in the round. The Christian life must be viewed as a journey, a pilgrimage of faith, hope, and love, in which no single waypoint, episode, or captured moment can hope to represent the whole. As pilgrims, we are the journey, but we are also the destination to which our shared faith impels us and in which we ultimately trust.

Rev. Kevin O'Brien
Church of Ireland Rector
St Columba's Church, Binden Street
Ennis, Co. Clare

Timeline of C. S. Lewis

1898	November 29, born in Belfast
1908	His mother, Flora Hamilton Lewis, dies
1917	Begins studies at University College Oxford Becomes soldier in World War I
1925	Elected a fellow of Magdalen College Oxford
1931	Faith conversion
1933	The Inklings are formed
1940	Publication of faith works
1950	Begins writing *The Chronicles of Narnia*
1954	Leaves Oxford to accept the chair of medieval and renaissance literature at Cambridge
1956	Marries Joy Davidman
1960	Davidman dies
1963	Lewis dies

Prologue

This book is an introduction to the life and work of C. S. Lewis, Anglican theologian, scholar, poet, novelist, and dramatist. He produced a phenomenal amount of work in his lifetime and his work brought him to the level of international recognition that we might today describe as celebrity status. Much of his work is still read and admired, especially his children's fiction. Dramatization of his children's work in *The Chronicles of Narnia* series of films has led to a resurgence of interest in Lewis.

I often tell people that as a student I went through phases when I devoted most of my reading hours to a recently discovered author and read every piece of their writing that I could lay my hands on. While in such a phase, one thinks that one will remain with that subject or person forever; however, one moves on and is thankfully spared excessive or obsessive fandom. I moved on in time from John Henry Newman, John of the Cross, Thérèse of Lisieux, Thomas Merton, and Lewis, too. That intangible something of their influence, however, remains forever, and it shows in my being drawn back to them at regular intervals since I first read their works.

There is a popular impression of Lewis as a tweed-wearing, pipe-smoking, and real-ale-drinking scholar. This view of him is due in great part to the depiction of him in the film *Shadowlands*. Those who knew Lewis debunk that image and write instead of a man who was delightful company and carried his scholarly talents lightly. His work mirrored that sense of delightful company from the moment I was first introduced to it. I would like nothing better than to introduce you, the reader, to Lewis so that you, too, might be enthralled by his company.

The C stands for Clive and the S stands for Staples. The latter, unusual name comes from the French word *estaple*, meaning marketplace. Used as a surname, it is thought to be that of a family who lived in the environs of a marketplace. It is said to have been brought to England after the Norman conquest in 1066. Lewis's father was a solicitor, and the family was reasonably well-off and belonged to middle-class Belfast ascendancy, compared to the much less well-off minority Catholic population.

There is no doubt that the tweedy, pipe-smoking, and real-ale-drinking scholarly aura around Lewis exists to this day. It causes many of us to look on him as so frozen in time that we cannot relate to him, and so we tend to move on from him because he is too far beyond our reach.

I have debated with myself this sense of remove from

Lewis and dared to question whether, as a Catholic, I suffer reservations regarding Lewis because he was a Northern Irish Protestant. Was this mild sectarian bias at work unconsciously in my own outlook and psyche? Like a lot of Catholics, I admired him but sometimes sidelined him because he was not a Catholic. One can say that people wished Lewis would have taken the final step and become a Catholic, like Newman.

Lewis was close to Catholicism and was influenced by his friend J. R. R. Tolkien, who was a Catholic. Lewis would have pleased his Catholic readership if he had converted. There was a conversion of sorts in his life in that he returned to Christianity at age thirty-two, having abandoned it in his early teens. He was an Anglican and remained one until his death. He had no desire to be any more than an Anglican. He was perfectly happy as an Anglican. I put my sectarian-bias issue to my Anglican friend Kevin O'Brien and asked him to address it in his foreword to this book.

When Lewis was a boy growing up in Belfast, his family had a Catholic maid, and that was the extent of his familiarity with anyone of a different creed. Lewis is said to have had no time for sectarianism — it seemed to him quite natural that Catholics and Protestants should coexist peaceably. To someone living in southern Ireland, because of birth and upbringing, Lewis might have come across as British rather than Irish, but he always regarded himself as Irish and was quick to point out that he had little in common with English people. It is ironic that despite his Irishness he was educated mainly in England and spent most of his adult life in two bastions of the British educational system — Oxford and Cambridge universities. He spent most of his adult life in England, with only occasional visits to Ireland, yet he always considered himself to be Irish and claimed his Irishness as the source of his creativity.

Creativity spurred by imagination was an important ingredient in Lewis the writer and thinker. He had this in common with his friend and fellow Oxford academic, Tolkien. In a sense, the idea of appearances belying the person is attributable to both Lewis and Tolkien. Both were academics and in their middle age when they published literary works of their imaginations. When you see photos of the sedate-looking Lewis and Tolkien, you would need to exercise your own imagination to see them as the authors of such imaginative works.

This is the beauty of imagination and its universal appeal — it is indigenous to humanity and requires no lively body, body beautiful, or other physical attributes to function. Perhaps the only requirement is for a person to activate it by a conscious exercise of the mind — that is in itself only a small thing to do — and we call it tapping one's imagination. It is as simple as turning on a tap. Of course, what comes out will be liquid gold for some and not as rich an elixir for others.

I would like to think that this work in appreciation of Lewis will do two things for you, the reader. First, reintroduce you to the inner journey of your own soul as you consider Lewis's apologetics. Second, stir up your own imaginative side as you reconsider the writings of Lewis the storyteller. In a sense, all his work asks his readers to be childlike, to return once more to the earlier years of childhood when all our worlds were simpler and richer places. In an introduction to one of his works, *Surprised by Joy*, he writes, "I never read an autobiography in which the parts devoted to the earlier years were not far the most interesting."

C. S. Lewis was a complex individual. He was a bright, precocious boy, a soldier, an academic, a lover, a creative and scholarly writer, and a man of faith — all rolled into one. I put it like that because it strikes me that Lewis always carried within him an awareness of all these aspects of his makeup. More than anyone, Lewis seems to have understood childhood's formative and lasting powerful hold on one's future. It is the key that unlocks the door in our quest for finding the inner life of our souls.

PEACE AT FIRST

CHAPTER ONE
Shaping the Man

The two families from which I spring were as different in temperament as in origin.[1]

A birth cry signals the beginning of a new life and is the infant's first vocal contribution to the world he or she is going to inhabit for a lifetime. It contrasts with the relative peace and calm of the womb and is an abstract acknowledgement that the previous accustomed peace is over, and the inherent search of a lifetime has begun — a search to find in this new life some semblance of that former peace, or at best a peace that will come close to satisfying the searcher.

Clive Staples Lewis made his birth cry on November 29, 1898, in Dundela, suburban Belfast, County Antrim, Northern Ireland. The family lived in a house called Dundela Villas. Whether he let out a loud or a mewling birth cry, he was born into a family of relative prosperity and comfort. He had little to cry about in material terms. His earliest years were marked by a sense of peace and tranquility. All the signs were that a happy childhood lay before him. However, his peaceful childhood years were shattered by his mother's death, and he spent a large portion of his life from that point forward attempting to rediscover the inner peace that had marked his early years with a sense of tranquility, happiness, and, in a unique way for Lewis, joy.

PARENTS AND FAMILY

His parents, Albert and Florence, were Protestant, and this religion was given a respected and rightful place in their lives, but they were not overly religious. Florence (née Hamilton) came from a line of Protestant clergy; her father was a rector and her grandfather had been a bishop. Florence was not the typical wife and mother of her class, even though she upheld the accepted wifely and motherly norms of the time. This conformity to social norms masked the fact that Florence was a highly educated woman who had been the recipient of an honors mathematics degree from Queen's University, Belfast. She is said to have held back in displaying her feelings more than her husband did. A letter from her to Albert during their courtship has a slightly quirky note of reticence that displays a sense of her reserve. She wrote, "I wonder whether I do love you? I am not quite sure."[2]

Albert was a police solicitor and highly respected in both his profession and within the gentleman class. This was accompanied by a creative side, often expressed in his public-speaking skills, recounting funny incidents, or "wheezes," as they were known within the family. He had some ambition to enter into politics, for which people thought his speaking abilities, honed in court presentations, made him eminently suitable. His aspirations for a life in politics did not come to fruition, and he settled in as a busy solicitor. He believed in God and saw church attendance as a necessary adjunct to personal faith, but religion was not a preoccupation of his life. He liked the outdoors and walking, a habit he instilled in his children.

After his wife, his great passion in life was literature, and he read voraciously a wide range of authors. He had a well-stocked domestic library, his books were precious to him, and he could be precious about them. There was an incident just a few months before the young Lewis was sent to the war trenches of France in which he spent a week with his father before returning to England. C. S. Lewis recalls borrowing a novel (*The Angel of Pain* by E. F. Benson) as reading material for the boat trip back to England. A short time later his father wanted the book returned, and Lewis wrote, "I will send you *The Angel of*

Pain in a few days."[3] Albert's concern that his book be returned was paramount and was not to be overlooked just because his son of eighteen happened to be going in a few months' time to the killing fields of France.

THE BROTHER

Waiting to welcome Clive Staples into the world of the Lewis family was an older brother, Warren, who was then aged three. It is remarkable that the two brothers never lost the close attachment to one another that was formed at the younger brother's birth. They had separate careers in life — Warren was a soldier and Clive a scholar and writer. Yet, they were never out of each other's lives because they maintained their close friendship through letter-writing and holidaying together; and, in 1932, Warren retired and came to live with Clive near Oxford until the latter's death in 1963.

Both brothers became better known to family and close friends by nicknames: Warren was Warnie, and Clive was known as Jack. Both names attached to them in childhood. At the age of three, Clive announced he was to be known as Jacksie after the death of a pet dog of the same name. It quickly evolved into Jack, and that lasted all his life. Their use of these familiar names, while not unusual, does reflect the closeness of the brothers from childhood.

Jack and Warnie had a sheltered childhood in that they didn't mix with many boys of their own class. Likewise, it would have been unheard of for children of their age to mix with lower- or working-class children. There were few prospects of Ulster Protestant children even meeting Roman Catholic children, let alone socializing with them.

C. S. Lewis wrote of his family's life in his autobiography *Surprised by Joy*, published in 1955. The subtitle of this work is *The Shape of My Early Life*, which is an indication of how he saw his life as shaped by strong influences such as family and schooling, and, most importantly, how his Christian life was once abandoned and later found. The word *shape* and its subsequent effects are a good way to describe the many twists and turns Lewis's life took from early childhood right through adult life and to the end of his life.

The world of the Lewis children was in many ways quite sheltered and, in some ways, isolated from the world. They were a private family, and the children rarely got the opportunity to engage in the rough-and-tumble routine of playing with other children. In some ways they were cocooned and got to exercise their imagination and childhood interests by way of reading and family discussion. Their lives were not dull, and they did not sense any negative restrictions on their boyhood happiness. They were surrounded by loving parents, a domestic servant or two, and a governess. The adults in their lives created a structure that was built on a belief that children absorbed influences within the home. They were left to their own devices once the necessary requirements of food, drink, clothing, early educational training, and attendance at religious services were provided by the adults in charge.

AT PLAY, TWO BOYS

In 1905 the family moved to a newly built house, with design direction from Albert, named Little Lea. It was an upwardly mobile move to a more fashionable area that was in keeping with both parents' belief in the expectations of their class. From the outset, the brothers were very happy in their new home, which presented them with ample scope to develop their imaginations in play and intellectual pursuits. The Lewis boys relied on their imaginations for play as children do, but they were more reliant on their imaginations simply because they didn't play or interact with other local children.

It was in this new house that the Lewis boys discovered the value of a playroom as not only an escape from parents and servants, but as an escape into the world of play with its promise of adventure steeped in aspects of the exotic, the fantastic, and the sheer joy of play. There was such a room situated in the attic of the house, which from the earliest moment the boys saw as their special den, or their boys' world, untainted by the demands and troubles imposed by adults on their everyday life. They called it the Little End Room.

It would be too easy to suggest that the Little End Room was the magic room of the Narnia wardrobe or that at that early age Jack had a sense of the room's future significance and importance. Its influence was probably from his subconscious, planted there in childhood. After the death of their father, he and Warren revisited the house, and both had a wistful sense of the room as representing a happier time and a childhood that had passed but which to some degree both had carried with them throughout life. In Jack's case, the Little End Room did to some extent underline the importance of the escapism of play and fantasy in a child's life — which was something he tapped into in his children's literature.

The happier time that both Jack and Warnie remembered was their earlier childhood, when their mother was still alive. Jack was only ten when she died suddenly. Though she had been ill, her death was still unexpected. Her death shattered her sons' idyllic childhood and, arguably, neither recovered from it. For Jack, who lived in the house throughout his mother's illness, her death was traumatic. Even though he knew she was very sick, it still felt like one moment she was there and the next moment she was gone. At the time, Warnie was in boarding school in England. He, too, remembered a home where she was a dominant presence. While away, his homesickness was always alleviated by the thought that he would be reunited with her on his next school holiday. When he returned home, it was to her funeral and the home would never be the same for him.

C. S. Lewis's experience of schooling throughout his childhood was an unhappy one. (Warnie did not altogether shine in the local school — but survived it better than Jack.) Shortly after his mother's death, Lewis was dispatched to Wynyard School, Hertfordshire, which Warnie had attended since 1905. After Wynyard closed in 1910, Lewis spent one term at Campbell College, Belfast, then went to Cherbourg House, the preparatory school for Malvern College in Worcestershire. The traditional model of schooling did not suit Jack at all. If anything, it seemed to stifle his natural abilities. It was clear that he was creative, curious, and imaginative — traits his mother would have encouraged. He and his brother were the sons of two very intelligent parents — a father in the legal profession who had literary leanings and a mother who had a mathematical qualification. There is no doubting the fact that he and his brother were gifted with an intelligence that was nurtured by their early reading, playful imaginings, and interest in the natural environment. They absorbed knowledge and their intellects were honed by their inquisitive interaction with the world around them.

Struggling with his own grief, their father Albert was incapable of attending to his sons' emotional needs after their mother's death. It was unusual to discuss grief at the time and it was encouraged to "keep calm and carry on." Albert simply saw them as requiring education in a secure and stable environment together. He arranged for Jack to join Warnie at his boarding school in England. Lewis was unhappy there and in subsequent schools. It was while at school in Cherbourg, Malvern (1911–13) that his faith finally withered away. He had come under the influence of a teacher, G. E. Crowe, who encouraged his interest in spiritualism, and he became disillusioned with Christianity. This was the result of several factors: a matron at school who introduced Lewis to occultism, his own struggles with prayer, and his reading in the classics. During this time, he struggled with various adolescent issues and found life difficult generally. It was also at Cherbourg that Lewis discovered Norse mythology and through it experienced a personal renaissance. He describes the overwhelming emotion and awe-inspiring escapism he felt when reading it. He also vividly describes the feeling of familiarity and sense of returning home that he experienced when reading Norse mythology:

> And with that plunge back into my own past there arose at once, almost like heartbreak, the memory of Joy itself, the knowledge that I had once had what I now lacked for years, that I was returning at last from exile and desert lands to my own country.[4]

This recurring experience of what Lewis alternately calls joy or longing is one of the factors that eventually led him back to faith in Christ.

After his youngest son had attended three different colleges in a short space of time, Albert made provision for him to come under the care of a personal tutor, William Kirkpatrick. Kirkpatrick was Albert's old tutor and headmaster of Lurgan College (known affectionately as the "Great Knock"); he was a very influential teacher and Lewis blossomed academically. He studied and lived with Kirkpatrick and his wife from 1914 to 1917. It sparked the beginning of a lifelong interest in the classics, debate, and logical argument. Lewis found in Kirkpatrick someone who challenged him intellectually and who sharpened his thought process. Kirkpatrick was what we might call a freethinker, and his broad approach to education seemed to suit Jack. Kirkpatrick was an atheist and his outlook helped Jack come to terms with his own evolving atheism. Kirkpatrick saw a career as an academic in Lewis's future, and their time together more than prepared him for Oxford. The only obstacle to his transition to Oxford was World War I, which was on the horizon.

Friendship was always important for Lewis, and his close association with Arthur Greeves was very much part of his story. Lewis and Greeves first met as young boys when they lived on the same street. Despite the close friendship of colleagues in Oxford and the Inklings, Greeves was Lewis's one constant and most loyal friend from early days until his death. Greeves, sensitive by nature, was a talented writer and an atheist. He was open about his sexuality, which no doubt was a challenge in the Northern Irish society of that time.[5]

IN SEARCH OF PEACE

CHAPTER TWO

A Place of Visions — Oxford

Amid life's chaotic dance of highs and lows, we all engage in a perpetual search for peace. The poet W. B. Yeats captures the mechanics of the search for peace when he writes, "I will arise and go now, and go to Innisfree."[1] Yet even in the ideal dream place, peace cannot be summarily plucked from the air, but it takes its own time, "for peace comes dropping slow."[2] C. S. Lewis, whose first literary calling was that of poet, had throughout his life a drive that reflected a great desire for peace. He began his search in earnest in his undergraduate years at University College Oxford and continued throughout his early teaching career there.

His early childhood was peaceful and idyllic. He experienced peace and joy and took it for granted in all that surrounded him — the joy of the playroom, shared sibling games, outdoor walks, and, of course, the developing imagination that brought him the joy of a fantasy world. This peace was shattered by his mother's death and from then on his childhood was disjointed. On the brink of adolescence he found himself cut off from a remote father who was himself immured in grief after the loss of his wife.

Lewis had lost the peace of his early childhood, and the travails of his secondary school education heightened that loss. If he was ever to regain a semblance of that former peace, he would first have to initiate a search for it. Once the search began, it would prove to be a long one that was punctuated by passing moments of joy, but nothing enduring would come on the horizon until much later in his academic and personal life. However, it was his arrival in Oxford that saw the search begin in earnest, and his poetic sensitivity enabled him to realize that elements of peace were to be found in the very act of searching itself. Oxford was to be the long-awaited, but slow to evolve, cathartic point in his literary, creative, spiritual, and personal life.

OXFORD

His mentor and tutor, William Kirkpatrick, believed that Lewis had the potential to have a career in law or literature. He saw in him a strong analytical mind and temperament suited to legal argument as well as to literary criticism. Kirkpatrick wrote to Lewis's father, saying, "It is the maturity and originality of his literary judgments which is so unusual and surprising."[3] Imbued with such gifts and a passion for learning, it might be said that Lewis was made for Oxford and that Oxford was made for him. They met each other's needs admirably.

He first visited Oxford for a scholarship exam on December 4, 1916, and was impressed by the academic atmosphere, the look of the historic buildings, and the aura of learning surrounding them. He won a scholarship to University College and the following April the dream of his life was about to come true as he began his university life reading classics.

Those first few months in Oxford were idyllic. He later wrote in *Spirits in Bondage* that Oxford was:

> A clean, sweet city lulled by ancient streams,
> A place of visions and of loosening chains,
> A refuge of the elect, a tower of dreams.[4]

The Oxford idyll was soon harshly interrupted as the reality of World War I began to be felt in the country and the university itself. Less than two months after arriving in Oxford, Lewis joined the army. This necessitated a change of lodging and he was removed to nearby Keble College, where he shared a room with another soldier, an Irishman called Paddy Moore.

NEW FRIENDS AND NEW FAMILY

Lewis couldn't have known that his meeting and subsequent friendship with Moore would be a life-changing moment that would greatly influence and affect the shape of his entire life to come. Moore did not enter Lewis's life alone, but brought with him his mother, Janie, and his young sister, Maureen. Janie Moore was separated from her husband. She was very close to Paddy, and whenever he moved, she moved. In modern parlance, we might say that the Moore family came as a package — if you got one, you got all three of them. At this time the family was living close by in Oxford.

It might be argued that Lewis was emotionally in need of a family unit, not to mention a maternal replacement for the mother he had lost early in life. He took an instant liking to the Moore family and spent whatever free time he had with them. It was a relationship that would grow in strength and mutual dependency from that point on.

The friendship between Moore and Lewis intensified when they became soldiers. In September 1917, Lewis was assigned to the 3rd Somerset Light Infantry. Both faced the daunting prospect of frontline action. While on leave during that time, Lewis stayed with the Moore family. The men made a pact that should anything happen to either of them during the war, the survivor would look out for the other's family. It was a pact that would copper-fasten the hold of the Moore family on Lewis and his connection to the family. His boyhood friend Arthur Greeves suspected very early on that Lewis's strong affection toward him was weakened by the arrival of Janie Moore.

THE WAR

The relentless demand of the war for more men (cannon fodder) meant that Lewis was dispatched to France in November 1917. He arrived at the frontline trenches on his nineteenth birthday. A few months later he succumbed to the blight of trench fever. In February 1918 he spent three weeks in hospital recovering before being sent back into action.

Like many who fought on the frontline of World War I, Lewis maintained a lifelong silence about his war experience. He had seen frontline action, fired and been fired upon, and was acquainted with both the mind- and physically numbing effects of trench warfare. Did it make him a pacifist? No. Lewis was a lover of peace in its many forms, but the outbreak of the war called him to action to defend his country. Much later, in World War II, Lewis was able to defend his country's need to go to war. He was never a warmonger, but he believed in upholding one's duty to one's country in its hour of need.[5]

The issues of war and peace are literally issues of life and death, and therefore the tragedy of war must never be forgotten or minimized. The horrors of war are surely the closest approximation there is to hell on earth. War changes lives forever in ways that are otherwise unthinkable. From a Christian perspective, war entails the death and killing of people who are all created in the image of God and, therefore, have inherent dignity and incalculable worth. And yet, even after experiencing war firsthand, Lewis believed war is sometimes justifiable and necessary.[6]

Lewis was one of those who faced the final German attack on the Western Front. He was injured badly and ended up in the hospital again. In May, he was sent to a military hospital in London where he received much attention and care from Janie Moore, who perhaps now saw him both as Paddy's friend and as another son. It behooved her to look after him in the absence of Paddy, who was also fighting at the front.

Her devoted attention highlighted for Lewis the detachment of his own father, who disappointed him by never coming to visit him during that time. September 1918 brought the news that Paddy Moore had been killed in action. It was only natural that Lewis was able to be of support and consolation to Janie Moore and Maureen in their bereavement. Lewis, the ever-dutiful and sensitive human being, would not have hesitated to honor the promise in the pact made with Paddy only a year or so before. It was perhaps too early for either Lewis or Paddy's mother to realize the truth that in her bereavement she had gained a new son, and that the motherless Lewis had now become an only son to a new mother.

BACK IN OXFORD

Reality was nearing the truth: In January 1919 Jack returned to Oxford. Janie Moore and Maureen moved to be even closer to Lewis. This habit of moving to be near Paddy had now established itself as moving to be closer to the "new" son. Jack was obliged to spend a year in residence in at the college, but he spent any free time he had with the Moore family. Once the year of required residence was up, Lewis had a joint household with the Moores, and he soon began to refer to this arrangement as "the family."

Throughout his time in the war, Lewis continued his lifelong love of writing, and he had a firm ambition to be first and foremost a poet. Writing was a fact of his life no matter where he was, and he wrote a collection of war poems that were published in book form as *Spirits in Bondage: A Cycle of Lyrics*. He was just twenty years old, and it looked as though he had a future as a writer.

The demands — and Janie Moore could be demanding — of his new domestic arrangements did not hinder Lewis's studies, and he performed brilliantly in all his exams, gaining many first-class honors awards in those years. The new family life brought stability to Lewis's personal life and its physical demands, such as household repairs and running errands, which acted as a happy counterbalance to his mental engagements in the academic world. Lewis was happy to be an errand boy — and, as many believed, Moore's lover — and a man of letters.

Lewis was on the way to fulfilling his ambition of an academic career, and by 1924 he was being gradually integrated into the staff of the college. The following year he was elected to a fellowship in Magdalen College in English —not philosophy as he and others might have anticipated. Lewis was at home in either the faculty of philosophy or English. His father's early influence on his literary life and Kirkpatrick's emphasis on philosophy made him eminently suitable for the study of either.

CONVERSION TO FAITH

The strain on the relationship between Lewis and his father began to ease with the deterioration of his father's health. He suffered from severe rheumatism and was later diagnosed with cancer. Albert James Lewis died in 1929. Neither Warnie nor Jack ever really forgave their father for his detachment from them at the time of their mother's death. It strikes the modern mind as cold and impersonal, but his detachment reflected the emotionally constricted norms of the father–son relationships of the time. The more sensitive Jack spent a lifetime coping with the alienation he felt existed between his father and himself. They did relate reasonably well to each other in Albert's latter years, but it was never going to be a joyful relationship. Albert respected, admired and was proud of his son's achievements, but in his world these sentiments were best felt, thought about, but not expressed.

Prompted by his father's illness, Lewis continued his search for meaning and the possibilities of a life of faith. He had rejected the faith of his parents, the faith of his schooling, which was the established Church of England brand of Christianity. He discussed issues of faith with close friends, and their reading of G. K. Chesterton's *The Everlasting Man* led him to experience the beginnings of what he thought to be a life of faith. In *Surprised by Joy*, he famously describes his eventual conversion: "I gave in and admitted that God was God, and knelt and prayed: perhaps, that night, the most dejected and reluctant convert in all of England." Initially, this conversion was to a form of "theism" — a basic acceptance of a belief that God exists. Later, following in-depth discussions with his friends Hugo Dyson and J. R. R. Tolkien, he came to know Jesus Christ as the son of God. His faith had taken on the dimension of a personal relationship.

THE KILNS

Around that time (1930) Jack and Janie Moore ("Minto," as the Lewis brothers referred to her) purchased a country residence called The Kilns with nine acres of land that was to become the home they had dreamed of. Jack and Warnie both contributed a share of the cost of The Kilns, with Moore paying her share. An agreement was made that it was to be home to the new family of Janie Moore, Maureen, Jack, and Warnie. In the event of the brothers' deaths the property would be owned by Moore.

Moore blamed God for the death of her son and was less than impressed with Jack and Warnie's newfound faith and their trips on Sunday mornings to worship in the local church; however, it was a tension that she learned to live with.

THE INKLINGS

Lewis enjoyed the camaraderie of male company, and for over thirty years a group of friends that became known as the Inklings met regularly to talk, drink beer, and share the fruits of their readings and recent compositions.[7] The gregarious Lewis enjoyed the company and the Inklings' gatherings gave a focus to his writings. It was an astute group in which he could bounce his literary ideas off and be inspired by them in turn. The therapeutic nature of writing for Lewis is summed up in a letter he wrote as a mere seventeen-year-old to Greeves, who was feeling poorly: "Cheer up, whenever you are fed up with life, start writing: ink is the great cure of all human ills, as I have found out long ago."[8]

Members of the Inklings included Owen Barfield, Tolkien, Dyson, and Charles Williams. The Inklings influenced Lewis by aiding his thought process as well as presenting him with astute and well-founded criticism. Warnie, who was a writer himself, joined them occasionally, and others drifted in and out of the company.

TUTOR AND LECTURER

Lewis's life became busier during his academic career.

He fulfilled the roles of college tutor, university lecturer, and literary historian. He was a popular tutor; his mix of good humor and concern for his students gained him respect and affection. Being a good speaker, he became one of the most popular lecturers at Oxford and drew large crowds when he spoke. During those years, along with his standard academic publications, he published literary works like *The Pilgrim's Regress* (1933), *The Allegory of Love* (1936), and *Dymer* (1926). From 1938, he published a science fiction series, The Space Trilogy, the first of which was *Out of the Silent Planet*, followed in later years by *Perelandra* (1943) and *That Hideous Strength* (1945). These initial fictional works were greeted with mixed reaction; it was only in later years that they gained more traction.

WAR AGAIN AND THE BIRTH OF AN APOLOGIST

With the start of World War II, Janie Moore and Lewis opened their home to schoolgirls evacuated from London, who came to live with them at The Kilns. Warnie was recalled to service. While Jack waited to see if he would be called up, he continued teaching at Oxford in circumstances restricted by the war.

Inspired by discussions and debates with the Inklings, Lewis started writing *The Problem of Pain*, a work he dedicated to the Inklings. The book opens with the line: "Not many years ago when I was an atheist." This was his first work of theology, and readers with a religious interest were now introduced to his scholarship and imaginative creativity. A new apologist had arrived on the scene.

FAITH IN TWENTIETH-CENTURY BRITAIN

Agnosticism had taken a firm hold of twentieth-century Britain. Academically, people of faith in England relied on biblical scholarship, which was going through a crisis partly because of the era of the "prophets of enlightenment," which brought the ideas of people like Darwin, Marx, Nietzsche, and Freud, to all of whom Lewis would have been introduced by his mentor and teacher Kirkpatrick. Modernism and its links with biblical criticism, the quest for the historical Jesus, and the "absolute idealism" of Hegel were all part of the ferment in which Lewis was taking an interest around that time.

Traditional Christianity still had some credible defenders in the intellectual milieu of the time, such as Ronald Knox, Chesterton, William Temple, and T. S. Eliot. However, drumming up interest in matters religious in Britain at that time was somewhat of a Sisyphean task, one which Lewis was willing to embrace.

CHAMPION OF ORTHODOXY

Lewis, at one stage, described his intellectual or faith journey as "a progression from Popular Realism to Philosophical Idealism; from Idealism to Pantheism, from Pantheism to Theism and from Theism to Christianity."[9]

Lewis's growing interest in Christianity was contested and questioned by his colleagues of a more liberal theological view. Those who knew him well expressed surprise at his conversion — especially when *The Pilgrim's Regress* was published in 1933. Commenting on remarks that college personnel were surprised to see Lewis in the chapel regularly, Eliot, who was no fan of Lewis, is reputed to have sarcastically said, "It's quite apparent that if anybody in an Oxford college wishes to escape detection, the one place for him to go is the chapel."[10] Little attention has been paid by commentators to Lewis's weekly practice of going to confession with his spiritual director, Fr. Walter Adams.

Lewis was driven by his conviction that Christianity is an objective fact and, though it may be difficult to comprehend completely, it is worth pursuing. His famous statement sums that up: "Christianity is a statement which, if false, is of no importance, and, if true, of infinite importance. The one thing it cannot be is moderately important."[11]

Lewis often saw himself in the role of what he termed a "translator," putting Christian doctrine into the vernacular or into language people could relate to and understand. In the early 1940s, it was precisely because of his natural gift in this area that the BBC invited him to present a radio series called "Right or Wrong: A Clue to the Meaning of the Universe." The series was hugely popular and heard by millions. It was the springboard for many similar radio talks by Lewis, as well as many speaking engagements and several publications. Quite a number of his talks were delivered to the Royal Air Force around that time, probably due to his military training and experience of war. His series on the subject was published in a newspaper and later became *The Screwtape Letters* (1942).

Lewis the academic was stepping outside the bounds of Oxford and engaging with a new audience. Inevitably, his fellow academics criticized him for what to them seemed to be an abandonment of the high ground of academe for the more popular halls and private homes where the general public were to be found. Perhaps, too, there was an element of jealousy in their criticism of Lewis, who was fast becoming a celebrity, which was anathema to the quiet authority immured in the halls of academe.

LIFE AT THE KILNS

Warnie returned from the war and, with Maureen's marriage to Leonard James Blake, there was enough space at The Kilns for him to have a room and an office that he used profitably to act as Jack's secretary. This involved answering the huge volume of fan mail that now arrived daily. Jack prided himself on answering most if not all his correspondence by return post.

Moore became more and more frail. Jack came under increasing pressure to care for her and cope with his busy routine. A series of maids were hired, but invariably Moore fought with them and, as a result, they didn't stay for long. Fred Paxford, the gardener and general factotum, whom Moore liked very much, was the exception to this rule.

Jack continued his lecturing circuit and producing radio series and various publications until 1943 — despite increasing domestic pressures. In 1944, Janie Moore had a stroke and lost power of one arm. Her decreasing health became a strain on Lewis, who was recovering from an operation to remove some wartime shrapnel that had been bothering him for many years.

INFLUENCE OF THE INKLINGS

Between his various publications, a series called "Beyond Personality" on the BBC, preaching at Oxford, and debates with the Socratic Club (college debating society), Lewis continued to enhance his reputation so much that he was being dubbed "the modern Oxford's Newman."[12] Lewis was an exceptional orator and an impressive debater. He had the great gift of being able to think on his feet. He had a photographic memory and could recall quotations or large passages of script verbatim.

The Inklings continued to meet and share literary ideas. Charles Williams was emerging as a fatherly figure amongst them during these wartime gatherings. He arranged a meeting between Lewis and Eliot in autumn 1944. As he expected, the chemistry between them was not good. Charles Williams' sudden death, just as the war was ending, was a huge blow to each member of the small, intimate literary group and had a profoundly sad influence on their gatherings for quite some time.

THE AFTERMATH OF THE WAR

Life was difficult in Europe after the war; in England,

with rationing in place, it took a while for the economy to get back on its feet. Lewis continued to work as hard and perhaps harder with his dedication and commitment to teaching, lecturing, debating, publishing, preaching, his radio series, looking after Moore, and an occasional jaunt away with Warnie into the countryside. In 1945, the University of St. Andrews took the unusual step of honoring Lewis, a lay theologian, with a Doctor of Divinity, which Lewis relished. In some accounts, Warnie appeared to be resentful that Jack dedicated the honor to Moore. Heretofore, Warnie had a good relationship with Moore, but this award seems to have been the cause of an alienation between the brothers, who had always been very close.

CHAPTER THREE
The Inner Child

No book is really worth reading at the age of ten which is not equally — and often far more — worth reading at the age of fifty and beyond.[1]

Even though he only began writing children's books late in life, C. S. Lewis's *The Chronicles of Narnia* transformed the world of children's literature. Most people today, if asked what Lewis meant to them, would answer with a single word, such as Narnia or Aslan. Likewise, if one said either of those words, most people would immediately know that you refer to the children's books that have become Lewis's lasting legacy.

Throughout his life, Lewis had little contact with children. During World War II, with the evacuation of children, some were relocated to The Kilns, and he seemed to get on reasonably well with them. He viewed their needs as more than simply material. He wanted them to discover their imaginations and, from his teaching experience, he knew that storytelling was a great teaching tool. Doubtless, this experience with evacuees influenced his writing for children. He probably saw that there was a dearth of good children's literature, and, in typical Lewis fashion, he knew he was capable of doing something about it.

It was more than the war-children, however. Deep within Lewis was the child of the secret playroom in his childhood home. He was always writing for that child. In effect, Lewis, like so many writers, was writing for himself. Much of thc inspiration to compose children's literature arose from conversations at the weekly Inklings gatherings and specifically from conversations with his great friend Tolkien. Both men were scholars of standing and wrote fiction as a sideline to their professional duties.

Tolkien's make-believe world was one of high fantasy, populated by hobbits, dwarves, wizards, and goblins. It appealed to children, and to adults for whom fantasy was a chosen form of escapism. Narnia was the make-believe world that Lewis created for *The Chronicles of Narnia*, a series of seven books that he wrote between 1950 and 1956. He invited the reader to enter a world of fantasy where there was an eclectic mix of talking animals, giants and dwarves, fauns and nymphs. One might expect that there existed a great deal of mutual encouragement between the two men. There was encouragement, but it was one-sided. Lewis affirmed Tolkien in his writing and urged him to persevere with his work. It's possible that without Lewis's encouragement Tolkien's work may not have seen the light of day.

Tolkien, on the other hand, did little to encourage Lewis's fiction and was openly critical of *The Chronicles of Narnia*. Tolkien had very strict standards when it came to writing his own fiction. He demanded accuracy in the backstory, history, and facts, all of which took a great deal of time to complete. He felt that Lewis's stories were too hastily written, contained too many inconsistencies, and were a hodgepodge of many different traditions and mythologies. Rowan Williams refers to Tolkien's reservations regarding Lewis's stories:

> Notoriously, Lewis's friend, J. R. R. Tolkien, found them intolerable. He hated the random mixture of mythologies (classical Fauns and Dryads, Northern European giants and dwarfs, and, to add insult to injury, Father Christmas) and the failure, as he saw it, to create the kind of fully coherent imaginative world that he had spent his energies on for so long.[2]

A reader might question why busy and serious academics like Lewis and Tolkien would invest so much of their spare time in the composition of children's literature, delving into the world of fantasy and science fiction. There could be a number of reasons why they did so, but an obvious reason should not be overlooked: They wrote children's fiction because they were able to, as talented storytellers with incredible imaginations. Both men had a natural gift for writing, and the sales of their books to this day are proof of that.

Lewis was a professor of English literature of the Middle Ages and philosophy, while Tolkien was an expert in the study of languages (philology) and specialized in ancient Norse language. Their academic fields of interest were fertile ground for anyone who had a vivid imagination and was drawn to a world of fantasy. Even though they were both interested in creating a world of fantasy and populating it with inhabitants of their own creation, their style of writing was very different.

Tolkien was the consummate academic and brought the academic approach of meticulousness and consistent research to his fiction. Lewis was freer in his approach and could leave aside the bounds of academic scholarship when he felt like it. Lewis was the more adventurous of the two and sensed that the child reader could be gripped by the excitement of a story and its interesting characters and setting. Creating this hook and instant escapism was more important than the rules of research that Tolkien held as sacrosanct. The work of neither man suffered because of their individual approaches to writing. Tolkien and Lewis were capable of making great leaps of imagination but approached the leap in different ways. Tolkien made a measured approach that entailed a long run up to his leap. Lewis was more joyous, and his leap of imagination was more spontaneous, which shows in his writing.

Lewis's great works of fiction have made a lasting impression on generations of readers, young and old. One critic described this work as "a blend of magic, myth, and Christianity, some of it brilliantly fantastical and richly imaginative."[3] There cannot be one reason alone that brought him into the world of make-believe, the planets and fairy tales, the world of walking trees, naiads, fauns, satyrs, dwarves, giants, centaurs, talking beasts. Some ask whether it was his friendship with Tolkien that triggered his desire to write.

It may have been a number of reasons, one of which is that Lewis simply enjoyed creating stories. Another is that his children's fiction was a vehicle back to the lost happiness of his childhood — those happy days in which he and Warnie immersed themselves in books that captured their imaginations. Lewis addresses the question of a writing plan in "Sometimes Fairy Stories May Say Best What's to Be Said," where he writes:

> Some people seem to think that I began by asking myself how I could say something about Christianity to children; then fixed on the fairy tale as an instrument, then collected information about child psychology and decided what age group I'd write for; then drew up a list of basic Christian truths and hammered out allegories to embody them. This is all pure moonshine. I couldn't write in that way. It all began with images; a faun carrying an umbrella, a queen on a sledge, a magnificent lion. At first there wasn't even anything Christian about them, that element pushed itself in of its own account.[4]

It might seem that this is our answer: He had no plan; it was all spontaneous creativity. This is confirmed somewhat in "It All Began with a Picture," an essay he wrote in 1960 in which he explains that once Aslan, the lion, bounded into the first book in the Narnia series, *The Lion, the Witch and the Wardrobe*, "he pulled the whole story together, and soon he pulled the six other Narnian stories in after him."[5]

Lewis does contradict this version of events elsewhere, notably in a letter to Anne Jenkins on March 5, 1961, in which he explains that the "whole Narnian story is about Christ."[6]

Lewis was deeply Christian and did say that "Aslan is profoundly Christ-like." Equally, the series is seen by many as entirely about Christ, with an obvious theological theme running throughout. Some commentators have gone so far as to make comparisons between the seven books and the Seven Deadly Sins, the Seven Sacraments and the Seven Works of Mercy of Catholic Church teaching. Christian themes abound in *The Chronicles of Narnia*, as Lewis himself explains:

> *The Magician's Nephew* — the story of creation and the arrival of evil
>
> *The Lion, the Witch, and the Wardrobe* — crucifixion and resurrection
>
> *Prince Caspian* — restoration of pure religion after a period of corruption
>
> *The Horse and His Boy* — the calling and conversion of a heathen
>
> *The Voyage of the Dawn Treader* — the spir-

itual life (Reepicheep, in particular)

The Silver Chair — the continued war against the powers of darkness

The Last Battle — the coming of the Antichrist (the Ape), the end of the world and the last judgement[7]

Christian believers have tended to hijack the series because of these religious themes. Lewis's ambiguity about their Christian content lies perhaps in a natural tension between the secular storyteller and the man of faith — Lewis was both. It's possible that he didn't want to ever lose sight of the fact that a person did not have to be a person of faith in order to read and enjoy *The Chronicles of Narnia.*

Most Lewis fans would suggest that a reader coming to the Narnia series for the first time should read them as entertaining children's stories — there's so much to enjoy, including the characters, the setting, the dialogue, and all that happens in the fantasy world created by Lewis — instead of concentrating on deciphering any theological message or hidden meaning. Lewis was not a theologian but a good storyteller, and in the process of telling a story he did discover the power of the medium to throw light on personal faith in both a covert and overt manner.

Many children's writers create interesting child protagonists or a cast of central characters around which their story is built. It is a tried-and-tested literary device that ensures the young reader will be drawn into the story from the outset. (Enid Blyton's *The Famous Five* and *The Secret Seven* series spring to mind.) Lewis created relatable and credible child characters in each of his books. The four Pevensie children — Peter, Susan, Edmund, and Lucy — are the main characters in the most famous of the books, whose wonderfully alluring title — *The Lion, the Witch, and the Wardrobe* — captures the reader from the first glimpse. Lucy is the most well-known of the four and was an inspiration for many young readers. Her courage and bravery as well as her keen sense of justice remain inspirational to new readers of the series.

The four children are sent away as evacuees from the war to a boarding school in the house of Professor Kirke. This draws on Lewis's own experience of being sent away to school and eventually ending up in the home of his mentor–teacher of a similar name, Kirkpatrick.

The children play a game of hide-and-seek. Lucy hides in an old wardrobe, which is a portal to another world called Narnia. Inspired by mythology and other classic stories, Lucy goes on a hero's journey. The story unfolds intriguingly as a faun called Mr. Tumnus explains the world of Narnia to her, taking on the role of mentor. It is ruled by a wicked White Witch called Jadis who has cast Narnia into the eternal darkness of winter. It is the stuff of children's storytelling at its best and one can see the emergence of the allegorical Christian landscape from the outset. Is the eternal darkness the world of sin and is Jadis the devil?

Then Edmund comes to Narnia and encounters Jadis, who offers to make him a prince if he brings the other children to her. You can sense the amalgam of ideas, themes, and allegorical references with which Lewis was fond of loading his stories, and which irritated Tolkien. As a writer, Lewis lets his imagination loose on the story and allows it a life of its own.

He has no hesitation in creating characters to match the flow of his imagination, and so he throws in characters like Mr. and Mrs. Beaver, who tell the children about Aslan, the great lion and king of the wood who has returned to Narnia to overthrow the White Witch, fulfilling an ancient prophesy that he would overthrow her when four sons of Adam and daughters of Eve are present on the thrones of the kingdom. Even the least discerning of readers will note that as the story evolves it becomes redolent with Christian allegory.

Christian symbolism continues throughout, right to

the end of the story. Despite Jadis' best (worst) efforts, the children join forces with Aslan, and many battles and intrigues follow. At one point, the White Witch prepares to kill Edmund for his treachery of abandoning her. However, Aslan offers his life in sacrifice and is slain. Aslan miraculously rises from the dead and returns. He brings good news of the "deeper magic from the dawn of time," that if a willing victim who has committed no treachery is killed in a traitor's place, death itself will begin to work backward. The good forces join Aslan in defeating the White Witch, and the children are crowned kings and queens of Narnia, where they reign for many years until they return to this world through the wardrobe.

If he never wrote another book in the series, Lewis had a success on his hands with the first, *The Lion, the Witch, and the Wardrobe*, which has been adapted for film and television, most recently in 2005. The following books were also a success and sold well, with two others later adapted for film, *Prince Caspian* (2008) and *The Voyage of the Dawn Treader* (2010). Little did Lewis know that the Narnian Chronicles would in time become a multimillion-dollar industry, selling over a hundred million copies in forty-seven different languages. During his lifetime, it made Lewis a wealthy man.

AT PEACE

CHAPTER FOUR
Man of Faith and Apologist

Apart from his successful children's literature, Lewis is most remembered as an apologist. The word *apologist* is not one which we are very familiar with today. It is a word that doesn't sit easily in our contemporary world, which is more assertive and brash in its views.

In terms of religious faith, the apologist means someone who is both a protector and a defender of his or her beliefs. Lewis built up a significant literary, lecturing, broadcasting, and public-speaking output that constitutes in its entirety what we call his apologetics.

The apologist was much respected, and even revered, in Lewis's day. Catholics of that generation will remember that apologetics formed part of their religious instruction at post-primary school. It was at that level of secondary school during his adolescent years that Lewis's childhood faith failed him.

The failure had set in even earlier at the age of ten with the traumatic loss of his mother. At the time he was separated from Warnie, who was away at secondary school in England. His own father's remoteness put Lewis in need of a substitute father figure. A child who had such a fertile imagination, who loved magic and fantasy, was most likely curious about the world of religion and might have turned to prayer.

Before long Lewis was sent to boarding school in England. In 1911–13 his already weakening faith in the conventional Christian God simply withered away, and he gradually came to see himself as an atheist.

It was while he was under the tutelage of "The Kirk" (Kirkpatrick) that Jack first read the novel *Phantastes*, which had a profound effect on his religious imagination. *Phantastes* is a fantasy novel by the Scottish writer George MacDonald, first published in London in 1858. The work, taking its inspiration from German Romanticism, centers on a character called Anodos, Greek for "ascent" or "pathless," who is pulled into a dream world where he hunts for the ideal of female beauty, embodied by the Marble Lady. He encounters many adventures and temptations before returning to the real world and giving up on his ideals. Ironically for Lewis, reflecting on this work sowed the seed for his future return to Christianity, and he wrote about the novel: "That night, my imagination was, in a certain sense, baptized; the rest of me, not unnaturally, took longer. I had not the faintest notion what I had let myself in for by buying *Phantastes*."[1]

Despite this initial step in the direction of a return to faith, he remained antagonistic toward, and well outside, the faith into his twenties, and could in terms of religious belief be described as fitting the category of an angry young man. Two of his earliest works, *Spirits in Bondage* and *Dymer,* give a sense of his antagonism and lack of enthusiasm for the Christian faith and God.

After World War I, Lewis took on a teaching role at Oxford. This happy reunion with academic life and his beloved Oxford did much to soothe the trauma he suffered from his battleground experiences. Lewis's search for meaning and truth resurfaced in the rarefied though secure atmosphere of college life. Many see it as a serious knocking on the door of faith, but it was, in fact, some time before he would even arrive at that door.

Lewis's close friendship with Tolkien, as well as a number of significant books he read, were a strong influence on him. Tolkien was a devout Catholic, and many thought Lewis would become a Catholic as well. But when Lewis finally made his act of faith, he did so as an Anglican. He was both proud and happy to be one, and while friendly with lay and clerical Catholics, he never looked on the possibility of a conversion to Catholicism as an option to be considered.

Lewis was a man who valued friendship, and he welcomed the diversity of his friends' opinions. It somehow increased his intellectual delight that his devout Christian friends (Inklings members Tolkien, Dyson, Barfield, Arthur Greeves, and others) could engage with him in respectful though often heated debate on religious topics. Lewis lived among devout believers — "Everyone and everything had joined the other side," he wrote — but he reveled in this fact and never saw his discussion with Christian friends as their arm-twisting him into belief in God. At this time before his conversion, one might describe Lewis as a devout and nonmilitant atheist.

A mix of writers influenced him during this time — some were firm believers in Christianity, others philosophical, and some he considered lacking in substance and would have benefitted from a faith perspective. We are talking of writers such as George MacDonald, G. K. Chesterton, Samuel Johnson, Edmund Spencer, and John Milton. It was in 1926 while reading Chesterton's *The Everlasting Man* that he felt the Christian perspective on history was starting to make sense. Still, at this point, he was ready to engage in battle against faith, and he refused to give in to it on the grounds that it was contradictory and unappealing on a personal level. He felt that "Christianity was very sensible 'apart from Christianity.'"[2] One senses that the intellectual Lewis was fearful of giving in to faith and thus reneging on his principles. He was, however, advancing on the road to faith. His colleague T. D. Weldon, a militant atheist, conceded in an argument with Lewis that the authenticity of the New Testament accounts of Jesus were amazingly strong. Following this, Lewis felt he was being trapped intellectually into acceptance of what he felt was the inevitable confession of faith.

Finally, his soul-searching came to an end. In 1929 Lewis gave in. He famously described himself as "the most dejected and reluctant convert in all of England."[3] He still didn't feel himself ready for a relationship with God. That was yet to come. His Damascus moment of conversion had to wait, as he still had much ground to cover in order to convince himself that it was good for him to be a Christian. On the evening of September 19, 1931, he dined with his friends Tolkien and Dyson. They spent the evening in deep conversation centering on myths and their truth or validity. According to Tolkien, the difference between myths and Christianity is that Christianity his a myth that actually happens to be true. This was a concept that the myth-loving Lewis could appreciate. He saw the conversation that night as an important conversion moment for him, writing:

> I was by now too experienced in literary criticism to regard the Gospels as myths. They had not the mythical taste. … If ever a myth had become faith, had been incarnated, it would be just like this. Myths were just like it in one way. Histories were like it in another. But nothing was simply like it. … This is not "a religion" nor "a philosophy." It is the summing up and actuality of them all.[4]

This epiphany happened a few days later while riding in the sidecar of his brother Warnie's motorcycle through the countryside. He finally made up his mind — he believed that Jesus Christ was the son of God. For Lewis, this point was more than an intellectual exercise, and his whole life was transformed. From that moment on, there was a new sense of joy and purpose to his life and work at Oxford. Much of his future years would be spent articulating and defending the Christian faith. Finally, he was ready to enter into that relationship with Jesus Christ and the joy associated with it. The sense of mystery he had as a child and lost had returned to him.

Lewis was a believer once more and prepared to live in a relationship with God for the remainder of his life.

THE EMERGENCE OF THE APOLOGIST

A standard definition of an apologist is, "a person who offers an argument in defense of something controversial." From what we know of Lewis, he would accept this as an accurate description of his work in this area. He was essentially a private man who liked to live in relative seclusion with his books and a few close friends. However, he was an intellectual giant and this, coupled with a natural gregariousness, propelled him to the fore whenever an intellectual clash of minds presented itself. In many ways it made him a natural apologist — one who could fight his corner. It must be said, too, that there was an inherent defensiveness in his outlook once he espoused Christianity again. He may have been embarrassed by his about-turn from convinced atheist to devout Christian. However, while his apologetic stance came from an initial personal defensiveness, his persistence and large output of works soon became a body of work that reached well beyond his fears and touched a much wider audience, who benefitted from his defense of Christianity for Christianity's sake alone.

Lewis was accustomed to lecturing and having full

lecture halls. By accident, during World War II, when he was invited to do a series of talks on faith matters for BBC Radio, he discovered that he was gifted in reaching a wider and more varied audience. Despite being an academic, Lewis had a gift for simplifying complex ideas and presenting them for radio in a witty and charming way. Gradually, his celebrity grew, much to the consternation of his academic colleagues, who felt that he had let down their side by crossing over to the world of plain minds — to put it mildly. Academic snobbery and bitterness was to follow Lewis all his life. His radio talks were published and widely read. He published other works on faith and practice, and by the 1950s he was well established as a renowned apologist or defender of the faith.

In 1954, toward the end of his career, Lewis accepted the newly founded professorship of medieval and renaissance literature at Magdalene College, University of Cambridge. This was a major departure for him, yet he maintained his strong links with Oxford. He returned to his home in Oxford on weekends, and this arrangement was in place until his death in 1963.

MERE CHRISTIANITY, 1952

Mere Christianity is a compilation of talks published in

1952. Many regard it as Lewis's most influential apologetic work. It is a concise summary, presented in an attractive, logical way, outlining the basics of the faith. Lewis's intent was to appeal to those who were skeptical about Christianity and whom he felt owed it to Christianity to examine its basic premises. This was his effort: to reach out to the academic world that rejected Christianity as an illogical choice. It was probably more the atheism of the academic world (including what was once a bastion of Christianity — see the Oxford Movement in Oxford itself) that made Lewis feel he had something to offer. He was already a respected academic and was trying to offer street cred from his newly acquired Christian perspective.

Mere Christianity begins with a description of Christianity as a big house with many rooms representing the many religious denominations. God breathes the air of his presence and life into every room. Lewis's intention was to present the house as a whole with all the undeniable truths therein. In four "books" it covers how we come to know God exists; the radical claims of Jesus; how God changes those who follow him; what it means to be a Christian and our belief in the Trinity.

LEWIS'S TRILEMMA

In addition to his awareness of the inclusiveness of language, Lewis is well known for his use of the trilemma argument, especially in *Mere Christianity*. He uses this argument in defense of the logic and rationality of the Christian faith and the divinity of Jesus. This argument is not unique to him, but it is perhaps he who popularized it the most. He states simply that Jesus had to be divine if he was not deluded or evil. It is sometimes described as the "lunatic, liar, or lord," or "mad, bad, or God" approach.

A strong feature of Lewis's apologetics was the understanding of universal morality, also understood as natural law, the inbuilt capacity that people have for doing right or wrong and encouraging others to do so also. Lewis maintains that all people can come to an understanding of this and abide by it if they choose to do so. He would argue that for such a law to exist there must be a greater design, or intelligence, behind it.

THE SCREWTAPE LETTERS, 1942

In the *Spiritual Exercises* of St. Ignatius of Loyola, the saint with a military background advises those serious about the spiritual life to know the tactics of the enemy well before going into battle. Lewis takes a similar approach in *The Screwtape Letters* in which he considers the world from the point of view of the devil. There is a combative air to this work that appealed to the readership of his day and continues to be popular today. The work follows the goings-on of a senior devil, Screwtape. He is in charge of a junior devil, his nephew, Wormwood, and instructs him in the art of temptation. It includes a collection of thirty-one letters from Screwtape to Wormwood, sharing tips and techniques on how to derail a person from the track of faith in Britain during World War II. It covers obstacles to faith: truthfulness, immorality, drifting from God, sinfulness, attractions of the world, selfishness, death, and many pathways that can drive a wedge between the person of faith and her or his God.

THE FOUR LOVES, 1960

Every year, when the texts on love from Saint John appear in the Church's office of readings, and in preparing a homily on the command of Jesus to love on Holy Thursday and throughout Eastertide, I'm invariably drawn back to *The Four Loves*.

In this work, Lewis divides the singular love, "that love which is God," into four quartets, using their original Greek description: *storge* (affection), *philia* (friendship), *eros* (sexual love), and *agapé* (charity). According to Lewis, three are human, or natural, loves, but *agapé* is divine love. God desires to infuse the natural loves with his love into the lives of the believer, to perfect these natural loves and raise them to a higher plain. They are all holy when God's hand is on the rein, but they can go to the bad on their own and can become false gods that lead one away from her or his true destiny.

Lewis makes a further distinction between "need-love" and "gift-love." Each of the four loves can be expressed in either of these two ways. Gift-love is selfless, reaching out to the other. Need-love responds to individual needs like a frightened child in its mother's arms. Even though gift-love is most godlike, Lewis does not attempt to portray it as being superior. After all, it is our need for God and God's love that motivates us to seek him in the first place.

TWIN SUCCESSES

Lewis achieved a fame he never desired on the strength of two separate activities — his apologetics and his children's books. He made a name for himself as one of the most talked about Christian apologists of his generation. When *Miracles* was published in 1947, *Time* magazine gave him the cover story. The associated article expressed surprise that such a noted academic would brazenly venture into the faith realm, going against the tide of the academia of the day.

Today, he is better known for his children's literature than for his religious writings. We are seeing a revival in religious and theological circles in the art of apologetics. It is perhaps a result of revisiting the Second Vatican Council and its experiential approach to faith. There are those who feel that the substance has gone from the teaching of Catholic doctrine since Vatican II. Lewis's apologetics provide a good starting point for those wishing to renew the content of faith and to make it palatable to those who seek an intellectual understanding of faith. It is good that Lewis provides this aid to faith for the modern searcher of truth, provided it is not at the expense of faith being lived out and found in what Patrick Kavanagh named "the bits and pieces of Everyday."[5] Lewis would have wished for such a happy union of the truth with the lived experience of the believer.

CHAPTER FIVE
Surprised by Another Joy

We soon learn to love what we know we must lose.[1]

Joy is a central motif in Lewis's life. It was something he experienced early in his childhood, and from that moment he would associate it with the idea of God. It was a special feeling that gave him a profound awareness of the extraordinary breaking into the ordinary moments of life. His loss of faith also led to a loss of joy, but on rediscovering faith he experienced joy once more in all aspects of living out his Christianity. It was so important to him that he named his autobiography *Surprised by Joy,* in which he wrote this about joy: "In a sense the central story of my life is about nothing else."

Coincidentally, joy was personified in Joy Davidman Gresham, who made a life-changing entrance into Lewis's life in 1950. In his settled, middle-aged bachelorhood, Lewis met, fell in love with, and married her. No one could have been more surprised than Lewis that he had fallen in love; to put it sentimentally, he was surprised by another Joy, who completed the joy that was already in his life.

Helen Joy Davidman was born in New York City in April 1915. Widely known as a poet and writer, she authored several books, including two novels, *Anya* (1940) and *Weeping Bay* (1950). *Smoke on the Mountain: An Interpretation of the Ten Commandments* is her best-known work, published in 1954. She had read and admired Lewis's writings, and her two sons were enamored with *The Chronicles of Narnia*. This American intellectual, writer, wife, and mother started a correspondence with Lewis, which he reciprocated. He enjoyed her intellect, wit, and humor. It would seem they were destined to be intellectual pen pals.

Destiny (or, as some claim, Joy) made other plans. Joy, at the time, was in a difficult marriage with her alcoholic husband, William Gresham, who was also a successful writer. Her correspondence with Lewis helped her. At a particularly difficult phase in her marriage, she felt the need to get away for a while. In 1952, she flew to England and found Lewis in the men's club in Oxford. She didn't know what he looked like but yelled out his name. He was pleased to make her acquaintance in person, at last. They got on well, and he introduced her to his friends and colleagues. It was to be a short visit. Lewis, while liking her and admiring her outspoken manner, probably saw it as a once-in-a-lifetime visit. Joy returned home, and they resumed their correspondence.

Was Lewis looking for a wife? Hardly, but did he need a wife? Probably, but the odds were stacked against his ever marrying. At the time he was a man's man: sociable, boisterous (boorish even); a beer-drinking, pipe-smoking, larger-than-life friend to his friends; and an inspiration to his students. He had found his niche in Oxford's academic cocoon and had pleasant public exeats from it to satisfy his interests. It would seem that he was content.

Nevertheless, despite the traditional male-dominated university environment in which he worked and the male friends he had, women played an important role in his life. His mother's death in his childhood was a major loss, and one he probably never quite got over. At any rate, he supplanted his mother when the first opportunity presented itself, especially in the case of Mrs. Moore. He more than fulfilled his promise to his friend Paddy, as he took her and her daughter into his life, and she had remained with him for the rest of her life. Jack referred to her as "mother," and Moore referred to Jack and Warnie as "the boys." It was a bizarre relationship, yet it seemed to fill some need in Jack. Much speculation has taken place as to whether he and Moore had a more intimate relationship than that of loyal care for the mother of a deceased friend.

That chapter of his life ended with her death in 1950; both his friends and Warnie felt that Lewis was at last liberated from the clutches of a domineering and demanding woman. Jack, too, felt the release from his duty of care to Moore and all it entailed, and he was happy to engage fully with academic life and the company of friends, and to live sedately with his beloved brother in the unobtrusiveness provided by that lifestyle.

The tranquil atmosphere of the Lewis household was disturbed in 1952 by Joy Davidman's return visit. Joy had fled her abusive spouse to live in England and taken her two sons, Douglas and David, with her. Lewis supported her financially while the family lived for a while in London and then moved to be near him in a home in Oxford. Both Joy and Jack had been on similar paths regarding faith and religion. Joy was of Jewish extraction, but like Lewis had lost her faith. Both she and Jack separately emerged from a period of atheism and searching, and both, as a result, became firm believers in Christianity.

There was some level of surprise, and disapproval,

of the relationship within his Oxford circle and close friends, especially in the established routine of the all-male Inklings club. As A. N. Wilson describes in his biography of Lewis, "Jack's other Oxford friends found the continual presence of Joy by his side irksome and baffling."[2] Despite this, Jack persisted in his relationship with Joy.

However, in 1956, Joy ran into issues with the civil authorities on the basis of citizenship, and Lewis offered to enter into a marriage of convenience to ensure she could stay in England. They were married privately in a civil ceremony, an occasion that Lewis later referred to as an "innocent little secret."[3] When news of the marriage leaked, to allay rumors and redress some of the disappointment of close friends (especially Tolkien) who were not party to plans for the occasion, the following announcement appeared in *The Times* on December 24, 1956:

> A marriage has taken place between Professor C. S. Lewis, of Magdalene College Cambridge, and Mrs. Joy Gresham, now a patient in the Churchill Hospital, Oxford. It is requested that no letters be sent.

After a happy first few years together, Joy was suddenly diagnosed with cancer and nearly died. This, however, proved to be the catalyst that brought the couple much closer and was the beginning of a deep and romantic relationship. Even though Joy was a divorcee, they had a religious ceremony of marriage at her bedside in 1957. The marriage was celebrated by a former student of Lewis's, Rev. Peter Bide, a Church of England clergyman. He went against the advice and wishes of his bishop, marrying them at Lewis's request. According to Alister McGrath: "Bide asked for some time to think about this request, which was in his view out of order. In the end, Bide decided he would do whatever Jesus Christ would have done. 'That somehow finished the argument.'"[4]

Miraculously, Joy went into remission, recovered, and for the next three years the couple lived happily at The Kilns. Joy transformed The Kilns from a bachelor pad that was rapidly falling into disrepair into an attractive home. She set about renovating, updating the furniture, and making all the necessary improvements. Tension arose with Maureen Moore, who made it clear to Joy that the rightful inheritance of The Kilns was hers. Joy expected that the property would go to her two sons.

In those years Jack started to fall head over heels in love with Joy. In a letter to Dorothy L. Sayers, he described this transformation from friendship to love, perhaps brought about by the shock and fear of losing Joy. He refers to Thanatos, the Greek god of death:

> My feelings had changed. They say a rival often turns a friend into a lover. Thanatos, certainly (they say) approaching but at an uncertain speed, is a most efficient rival for this purpose. We soon learn to love what we know we must lose.[5]

The Four Loves, which was written around this time, and some would view it as a joint effort between Lewis and Joy, explores this theme in more detail. The experience of this love in many ways transformed Jack. In some ways it softened his approach and attitude to life. He had, perhaps, lived in a more cerebral sphere until then. The few years that followed would seem to have been the happiest and most fulfilled of his life.

Warnie got on well with Joy. He stayed with them as a long-term lodger and continued to struggle with his lifelong challenge, his battle to be sober.

Sadly, in 1960, Joy's cancer returned. She and Jack went on one last trip to Greece, a measure of how much Jack loved her, because he hated traveling and only went in order to oblige her. Just three months after the trip, on July 13, 1960, Joy died. Her last words were, "I am at peace with God."

The death of his dearly beloved wife devastated and nearly destroyed Lewis. We get a sense of what she meant to him in his words:

> She was my daughter and my mother, my pupil and my teacher, my subject and my sovereign; and always, holding all these in solution, my trusty comrade, friend, shipmate, fellow-soldier. My mistress; but at the same time all that any man friend (and I have good ones) has ever been to me. Perhaps more.[6]

His loss was also poignantly expressed on her headstone:

> Here the whole world (stars, water, air,
> And field, and forest, as they were
> Reflected in a single mind)
> Like cast-off clothes was left behind
> In ashes yet with hope that she,
> Re-born from holy poverty,
> In Lenten lands, hereafter may
> Resume them on her Easter Day.[7]

A GRIEF OBSERVED

As was Lewis's practice in dealing with many things in life, he took pen and paper in hand and started writing as a form of therapy, to help himself deal with the situation. The result was a classic volume called *A Grief Observed.* The book was initially published under the pen name N. W. Clerk, to give him some anonymity while dealing with his personal anguish. It is a raw account of the grieving process and describes with great honesty his anger, sadness, and near despair:

> No one had ever told me that grief felt so like fear. I am not afraid, but the sensation is like being afraid. The same fluttering in the stomach, the same restlessness, the yawning. I keep on swallowing.[8]

It is also an account of his struggle with God and belief in the afterlife in the face of his tremendous loss:

> Meanwhile, where is God? ... But go to him when your need is desperate, when all other help is vain, and what do you find? A door slammed in your face, and a sound of bolting and double bolting on the inside. After that silence.[9]

Gradually, in the book, a sense of hope and an ability to cope slowly begin to emerge, and some glimpses of faith reemerged: "And so, perhaps with God. I have gradually been coming to feel that the door is no longer shut and bolted."[10]

When the book was published it was so effective that some friends actually recommended the book to him as a resource that might help him deal with the obvious sadness they had observed in him. It was only after his death that the book was finally published in his name.

THE SURPRISE OF JOY

It is beyond dispute that his friendship with and love for Joy transformed the latter years of Lewis's life. One might have thought at that stage in life a romantic adventure of true love might be beyond the realms of possibility for a cerebral academic who seemed content to remain a bachelor. Theirs was a true love story, with all the romance of the many fairy tales that Lewis penned, and which had such a profound influence on opening the minds and imaginations of many generations.

CHAPTER SIX

No Book Long Enough

Ink is the great cure for all human ills.[1]

Lewis had a keen awareness of the transitory nature of life. In the final weeks of his life, he wrote with an awareness heightened by final illness: "Yes, autumn is really the best of the seasons: and I am not sure that old age isn't the best part of life. But, of course, like autumn it doesn't last."[2] This prolific writer who loved books and found no book long enough had a strong hold on life while at the same time realizing that life itself was not an unending book.

For Lewis, writing was not just something he engaged in as a necessary tool for his academic work, but it was part of who and what he was. Writing, for him, was a form of therapy. His advice to his good friend Arthur Greeves as far back as 1916 was, "Whenever you are fed up with life, start writing; ink is the great cure for all human ills, as I have found out long ago."[3] After his wife's death, Lewis sought and found that therapeutic assistance in writing *A Grief Observed.*

By nature, Lewis was a very private man and did not venture into the realm of feelings and private emotions. *Surprised by Joy* and *A Grief Observed* were his two most emotionally charged works. He lived at a time when feelings were a private matter and expressing them on paper or in any public arena was seen as a sign of weakness. Feelings were better kept to oneself. It is true to say that despite his output of literary works, Lewis, like many writers, was not prone to giving of himself. To some extent this means that we never really get to know the real man behind the work. Nowadays, we are more inclined to expect our writers to "put themselves" into their work.

Lewis put himself into *Surprised by Joy* and *A Grief Observed*, and because of that, those two books have survived well and appeal to today's reader, who looks for that "bit more" from a writer. It was most likely Joy's influence that made him more sympathetic to the emotional side of life, by awakening in him the reality that human love was a gift from God, and that it, too, could be enjoyed and celebrated in the relationship between two loving people. It was this relationship that opened windows for him on the world at large and on areas of his own personal life. She also became his intellectual soulmate and encouraged him in his passion to continue to write. Her loss was deeply felt, but even in death she enabled him to plumb new depths within himself.

By the summer of 1961 it was clear that Lewis's health was in decline. In June he had a visit from his lifelong friend Arthur Greeves and described it as "one of the happiest times." However, in a letter to Greeves soon after the visit, he told him he was going to hospital for a procedure. Medical tests indicated that he was seriously ill and not well enough to have the procedure he had mentioned in his letter to Greeves.

He drew up his will, bequeathing his books and manuscripts to his brother, Warnie, along with any income arising from previous publications during the period of Warnie's lifetime. He struggled with the proportionate division of the remainder of the estate. Both he and his friend Tolkien came to the attention of the British revenue authorities in latter years and had large sums to pay as tax on book royalties. This came as quite a shock to Lewis, and it worried him considerably whether he would have sufficient means to cover these costs. As it turned out, there was a considerable surplus left in his estate.

Concern for Warnie's well-being was always uppermost among Jack's thoughts. Warnie was prone to more frequent bouts of alcoholism, despite his regular routine of treatment in the care of the nuns at Our Lady of Lourdes Hospital in Drogheda, Ireland. The Kilns began to deteriorate also in the absence and ingenuity of the house-proud Joy. Decline was all around Lewis. His friendship with Tolkien had deteriorated around this time, too, which only added to his unease.

Tolkien never encouraged Lewis's literary endeavors in children's literature, despite the fact that Lewis was hugely supportive and encouraging of him. Also, he was less than impressed at being kept out of the loop on Lewis's relationship with Joy and his marriage to her. It may have reflected small-mindedness on Tolkien's behalf. Lewis, however, rose above this and was generous enough to nominate Tolkien for the Nobel Prize for Literature in 1961 for his work on *The Lord of the Rings*.

In fairness to Tolkien, he didn't sever ties with Lewis, and upon his death he reached out to Lewis's stepson Douglas with an offer of help. The difference that may have existed between these two great writers was more in areas of disagreement over their craft as opposed to any personal animosity.

After Joy's death, her son David had a number of struggles in life and wasn't too involved in the affairs of the family. However, Douglas remained close to Lewis at all stages. A talented writer himself, he published an excellent book called *Lenten Lands* that gives a great firsthand account of the family background. Douglas and his wife spent a considerable number of years living in Ireland.

Between the years 1962 and 1963, Lewis lived in a state of declining health and spent less time in Cambridge. He befriended a junior American academic, Walter Hooper, who was working on a biography of him. Lewis invited Hooper to a meeting of the Inklings. He found that they shared a common interest in faith matters and in January 1963 Hooper agreed to become Lewis's personal secretary. Warnie's dependency on alcohol and increasing bouts of excess meant he was no longer able to keep on top of the ever-increasing secretarial workload.

In the summer of 1963 Jack suffered a heart attack and nearly died in the Acland nursing home, where he lay in a coma for some time. He recovered and returned eventually to The Kilns. There was a price to be paid despite the recovery: His delicate health forced him to resign his chair at Cambridge. His sole income at this point was the royalties from his books. All aspects of dealing with money continued to cause stress and anxiety for Lewis and did not get better as time went on.

Hooper had returned to the United States in the autumn of 1963, and Warnie eventually returned after his latest bout of alcoholism.

Lewis died on November 23, 1963, quite unexpectedly, after collapsing in his room. His death certificate listed renal failure, prostate obstruction, and cardiac degeneration as the causes of death. News of his death was completely overshadowed by President John F. Kennedy's assassination on the same day. Warnie, overwhelmed by grief, took refuge in alcohol, which added to the confusion and disorganization around the funeral arrangements to the extent that no public announcement was made. The funeral service was held on November 26 at Holy Trinity Church, Headington Quarry, Oxford, and was attended by a very small circle of his friends.

The verse chosen by Warnie for his brother's grave memorial was the verse from the Shakespearean calendar on the wall in their childhood home, Little Lea, that was open on the day their mother died: "Men must endure their going hence." This association with their childhood and its most traumatic event must have underlined Warnie's own ongoing sense of devastation — the great loss of a mother and now his beloved brother. Suffering had come full circle for Warnie, and the chosen verse probably gave no comfort to him, but only served to underline the misery he felt at the loss of his brother.

Warnie found none of the healing that Jack found in writing about Joy's death. Warnie sought to numb the pain with alcohol; this was to be his way of dealing with the terrible loneliness that losing Jack created in his life. He never recovered from the loss of his brother, and his heretofore bouts of sobriety became rarer in his remaining years. Warnie lacked the faith and hope that helped Jack ever since his rediscovery of the Christian faith. It served Jack well on the occasion of Joy's death, too, and he expressed it in words he penned a short time before dying. We are, he wrote:

> A seed patiently waiting in the earth to come up a flower in the Gardener's good time, up into the real world, the real waking. I suppose our whole present life, looked back on from there, will seem only a drowsy half-waking. We are here in the land of dreams. But cock-crow is coming.[4]

One might not be surprised at Lewis's popularity in the postwar era. People were searching in the aftermath of the war for meaning. They were interested in exploring religious faith. Then, in the 1960s, many became preoccupied with less abstract religious theories and more concerned with specific, practical issues that took center stage: human rights, the peace movement, racial issues, the sexual revolution, and other concerns. One would have thought that interest in Lewis was going into rapid decline from the 1960s on and that the years since then have proven him to be a man of his time.

Lewis is mostly associated in the popular mind with his legacy of children's books that have become popular through different forms of media: books, film, and television. However, he is still remembered for his contribution to the field of apologetics. Some of his apologetic works, like *Mere Christianity*, are still as readable as ever and remain direct, simple, yet comprehensive works covering the basics of the faith, and no doubt will continue to have a lasting appeal. Polls of American Christians have shown regularly that this work is among the most influential religious books of the twentieth century. *Mere Christianity*, *The Screwtape Letters*, *The Problem of Pain*, and *The Four Loves* were staples of my own religious formation, alongside the works of Newman and Merton.

Walter Hooper, who became his literary executor,

must be credited in no small way with keeping the flame of Lewis's memory and influence alive. Working in conjunction with Scottish publishers William Collins, Sons & Co., and with the establishment of the Fount imprint, a steady trickle of works appeared: *Screwtape Proposes a Toast* (1965), *Of This and Other Worlds* (1966), *Christian Reflections* (1967), *Fern-seed and Elephants* (1975), and *God in the Dock* (1979). The publication of Lewis's collected letters by Hooper in the immediate aftermath of the millennium added huge interest to the area of Lewis scholarship. Many good biographies also began to appear, and Lewis societies in the United States and England, along with various tours of interest in places associated with Lewis, all contributed to the enduring popularity of the man.

In his literary, imaginative works, Lewis stands shoulder to shoulder with the best in this field: Lewis Carroll, Kenneth Grahame, Rudyard Kipling, and the more contemporary Terry Pratchett, Philip Pullman, J. K. Rowling, and his lifelong friend, J. R. R. Tolkien.

Lewis draws on the imagination, fantasy, mythology, and the Christian faith to create a unique style that has been admired and respected by many generations of young readers and has done so much to promote and popularize the whole discipline of reading. *The Chron-*

icles of Narnia series has deservedly earned its place in the twentieth-century canon of children's literature. For Lewis, the only reliable measure of a writer's worth was the enjoyment one obtained from reading the works.

PEACE AT LAST

Clive Staples Lewis took his final leave of this world in a quiet and unobtrusive way. His death was noticed by only a few. His going quietly was in some ways consistent with how he lived. Despite his fame and influence, he liked nothing better than a cozy corner to read in, and a pub's snug in which to enjoy the company of good friends. His legacy of wisdom, knowledge, insight, and profound faith was to endure and bear much fruit and will continue to do so for many generations to come.

I feel that Lewis would look back on his own much-varied life and be happy with what he saw in it and count it as a blessing from God, a mixed blessing at times, but always a blessing. He would have no lingering regrets about the kind of person he was at various times throughout his life: teacher, tutor, professor, scholar, writer, philosopher, atheist, man of faith, man of prayer, apologist, children's author, fiction writer, friend, lover, husband, stepfather, and lover of nature. He lived out all these talents with a unique personal style that was richly seasoned with gregariousness, loyalty, and faithfulness, and which was fun-loving, intelligent, and studious. He would have deemed it a blessed life, which he tried at all times to live as blessedly as possible. I feel blessed that he did.

Poem for C. S. Lewis

AN ORDINARY MAN

Grounded, not hindered, by worldly cares:
Finding deeper significance in the domestic chore.
See-sawing between the extraordinary and the ordinary.
Finding contentment on being sent like a child on errands,
You come home laden with the fantastical and the wondrous.
A humble faith teaching you that imagination did not supplant the ordinary.
You knew and wished others to know it too:
Fetching a pound of butter was steeped in Mystery.

Notes

CHAPTER ONE: SHAPING THE MAN

1. *Surprised by Joy*, 1955.

2. A. N. Wilson, *C. S. Lewis: A Biography*, New York: W. W. Norton, 1990, 7.

3. *Lewis Papers* 5:229, quoted in Wilson.

4. Jessica Hooten Wilson, "C.S. Lewis's Mixed Bag of Tangents and Asides," *Church of Life Journal*, October 28, 2019.

5. An account of their friendship is documented in Walter Hooper (ed.), *They Stand Together: The Letters of C. S. Lewis to Arthur Greeves (1914–1963)*, London: HarperCollins, 1979. It provides a valuable insight into their individual concerns and the world around them during that time.

CHAPTER TWO: A PLACE OF VISIONS – OXFORD

1. W. B. Yeats, "The Lake Isle of Innisfree," *The Collected Poems of W. B. Yeats*, London: Wordsworth Editions, 1989.

2. Ibid.

3. *Lewis Papers* 4:256, quoted in A. N. Wilson, *C. S. Lewis: A Biography*, New York: W. W. Norton, 1990, 41.

4. *Spirits in Bondage: A Cycle of Lyrics*, 1919.

5. For more, see T.J. Demy, "A Dreadful Thing: C. S. Lewis and the Experience of War," *Sehnsucht: The C. S. Lewis Journal*, Vol. 5, 6, 2012.

6. D. Downing, "C. S. Lewis on War and Peace," *The C. S. Lewis*

Institute, https://www.cslewisinstitute.org/node/50.

7. The name "Inklings" could refer to a gathering of writers in advance of committing ideas to *ink* or of people sharing ideas around various *inklings*.

8. Letter of May 30, 1916, in Walter Hooper (ed.), *They Stand Together: The Letters of C. S. Lewis to Arthur Greeves (1914–1963)*, London: HarperCollins, 1979.

9. Preface to the third edition of *The Pilgrim's Regress*, 1943.

10. Arthur Hazard Dakin, *Paul Elmer More*, Princeton: Princeton University Press, 1960, 332.

11. Brian M. Williams, *C. S. Lewis: Pre-Evangelism for a Post-Christian World: Why Narnia Might Be More Real than We Think*, Cambridge, Ohio: Christian Publishing House, 2021, 208.

12. "Peterborough" in the *Daily Telegraph*, February 26, 1944.

CHAPTER THREE: THE INNER CHILD

1. *Surprised by Joy*, 1955.

2. Rowan Williams, in Introduction, *The Lion's World: A Journey into the Heart of Narnia*, Oxford: Oxford University Press, 2013.

3. Polly Toynbee, " Narnia represents everything that is most hateful about religion," *The Guardian*, December 5, 2005, https://www.theguardian.com/books/2005/dec/05/cslewis.booksforchi ldrenandteenagers.

4. "Sometimes Fairy Stories May Say Best What's to Be Said," *Of Other Worlds: Essays and Stories*, London: Harcourt Brace, 1966.

5. "It All Began with a Picture," *Radio Times*, July 15, 1960.

6. Letter to Anne Jenkins, March 5, 1961, in *Collected Letters, Vol. 3*, Walter Hooper (ed.), New York: HarperCollins, 2007, 1244–5.

7. Ibid.

CHAPTER FOUR: MAN OF FAITH AND APOLOGIST

1. *Surprised by Joy* in *The Inspirational Writings of C. S. Lewis*, New York: Inspirational Press, 1994, 100.

2. David C. Downing, *Planets in Peril: A Critical Study of C. S. Lewis's Ransom Trilogy*, Amherst: University of Massachusetts Press, 1992, 29.

3. ***Surprised by Joy***, 182.

4. Ibid.

5. Patrick Kavanagh, "The Great Hunger," *Collected Poems*, Antoinette Quinn (ed.), Allen Lane, 2004, 72.

CHAPTER FIVE: SURPRISED BY ANOTHER JOY

1. Letter from Lewis to Dorothy Sayers, quoted in Alister McGrath, *C. S. Lewis — A Life: Eccentric Genius, Reluctant Prophet*, Illinois: Tyndale House Publishers, Inc., 2013, 336.

2. A. N. Wilson, *C. S. Lewis: A Biography*, New York: W. W. Norton, 1990, 171.

3. Letter to Katherine Farrar, October 25, 1956, in *Collected Letters, Vol. 3*, Hooper (ed.), 801.

4. McGrath, *C. S. Lewis — A Life*, 336.

5. Letter to Dorothy L. Sayers, June 25, 1957, in *Collected Letters, Vol. 3*, 861–2.

6. *A Grief Observed*, 1961.

7. Appears as "Epitaph for Helen Joy Davidson" in *The Collected Poems of C. S. Lewis*, Walter Hooper (ed.), London: Fount, 1994, 252.

8. *A Grief Observed*.

9. Ibid.

10. Ibid.

CHAPTER SIX: NO BOOK LONG ENOUGH

1. Letter to Arthur Greeves, May 30, 1916, in *Collected Letters, Vol. 1*, Walter Hooper (ed.), New York: HarperCollins, 2004, 187.

2. Letter to Jane Douglass, September 31 [30], 1963, in *Collected Letters, Vol. 3*, 308.

3. Letter to Arthur Greeves, May 30, 1916, in *Collected Letters, Vol. 1*, 187.

4. Letter to Mary Willis Shelburne, June 28, 1963, in *Collected Letters, Vol. 3*, 1434.

Bibliography

WORKS OF C. S. LEWIS

Nonfiction

The Allegory of Love: A Study in Medieval Tradition, 1936.
The Problem of Pain, 1940.
The Case for Christianity, 1942.
A Preface to Paradise Lost, 1942.
Broadcast Talks, 1942.
The Abolition of Man, 1943.
Christian Behaviour, 1943.
Beyond Personality, 1944.
The Inner Ring, 1944.
Miracles: A Preliminary Study, 1947, 1960.
Arthurian Torso, 1948.
Transposition and Other Addresses (The Weight of Glory and Other Addresses), 1949.
Mere Christianity: A Revised and Amplified Edition, with a New Introduction, of the Three Books, Broadcast Talks, Christian Behaviour, and Beyond Personality, 1952.
English Literature in the Sixteenth Century Excluding Drama: The Completion of the Clark Lectures, Trinity College, Cambridge, 1944, 1954.

Surprised by Joy: The Shape of My Early Life, 1955.
Reflections on the Psalms, 1958.
The Four Loves, 1960.
Studies in Words, 1960.
The World's Last Night and Other Essays, 1960.
An Experiment in Criticism, 1961.
A Grief Observed, 1961.
Letters to Malcolm: Chiefly on Prayer, 1964.
The Discarded Image: An Introduction to Medieval and Renaissance Literature, 1964.

Nonfiction Collections

On Stories and Other Essays on Literature, Walter Hooper (ed.), London: Harcourt Brace, 1966.
Of Other Worlds: Essays and Stories, Walter Hooper (ed.), London: Harcourt Brace, 1966.
Studies in Medieval and Renaissance Literature, Walter Hooper (ed.), Cambridge: Cambridge University Press, 1966.
Christian Reflections, Walter Hooper (ed.), Cambridge: Eerdmans, 1967.
Spenser's Images of Life, Alastair Fowler (ed.), London: Cambridge University Press, 1967.
Letters to an American Lady, Clyde S. Kilby (ed.), Cambridge: Eerdmans, 1967.

Selected Literary Essays, Walter Hooper (ed.), Cambridge: Cambridge University Press, 1969.

God in the Dock: Essays on Theology and Ethics, Walter Hooper (ed.), Michigan: Eerdmans, 1970.

Fern-seed and Elephants and Other Essays on Christianity, Walter Hooper (ed.), London: Fount, 1975.

The Business of Heaven: Daily Readings from C. S. Lewis, Walter Hooper (ed.), London: Fount, 1984.

Present Concerns, Walter Hooper (ed.), London: Harcourt Brace, 1986.

All My Road Before Me: The Diary of C. S. Lewis 1922–27, Walter Hooper (ed.), London: HarperCollins, 1991.

The Latin Letters of C. S. Lewis, Don Giovanni Calabria (ed.), South Bend: St Augustine's Press, 1999.

Essay Collection: Faith, Christianity and the Church, Leslie Walmsley (ed.), London: HarperCollins, 2002.

Essay Collection: Literature, Philosophy and Short Stories, Leslie Walmsley (ed.), London: HarperCollins, 2002.

Collected Letters, Vol. 1: Family Letters 1905–1931, Walter Hooper (ed.), New York: HarperCollins, 2004.

Collected Letters, Vol. 2: Books, Broadcasts and War 1931–1949, Walter Hooper (ed.), New York: HarperCollins, 2004.

Collected Letters, Vol. 3: Narnia, Cambridge and Joy 1950–

1963, Walter Hooper (ed.), New York: HarperCollins, 2007.

Image and Imagination: Essays and Reviews, Walter Hooper (ed.), London: Cambridge University Press, 2013.

Fiction and Poetry

Spirits in Bondage: A Cycle of Lyrics, 1919.

Dymer, 1926.

The Pilgrim's Regress, 1933.

The Space Trilogy

Out of the Silent Planet, 1938.

Perelandra (aka *Voyage to Venus*), 1943.

That Hideous Strength, 1945.

The Screwtape Letters, 1942.

The Great Divorce, 1945.

The Chronicles of Narnia

The Lion, the Witch and the Wardrobe, 1950.

Prince Caspian, 1951.

The Voyage of the Dawn Treader, 1952.

The Silver Chair, 1953.

The Horse and His Boy, 1954.

The Magician's Nephew, 1955.

The Last Battle, 1956.

Till We Have Faces, 1956.

"The Shoddy Lands," 1956.

"Ministering Angels," 1958.
"Screwtape Proposes a Toast," 1961.
The Dark Tower, 1977.

Fiction and Poetry Collections

Poems, Walter Hooper (ed.), London: Harcourt Brace, 1964.
Narrative Poems, Walter Hooper (ed.), London: Geoffrey Bles, 1969.
Boxen: The Imaginary World of the Young C. S. Lewis, Walter Hooper (ed.), London: HarperCollins, 1985.
The Collected Poems of C. S. Lewis, Walter Hooper (ed.), London: Fount, 1994.
The Inspirational Writings of C. S. Lewis, New York: Inspirational Press, 1994.
The Collected Poems of C. S. Lewis: A Critical Edition, Don W. King (ed.), Ohio: Kent State University Press, 2015.

As Editor

George MacDonald: An Anthology, 1947.
Essays Presented to Charles Williams, 1947.

General Bibliography

Brown, D. *A Life Observed: A Spiritual Biography of C. S. Lewis*. Michigan: Brazos Press, 2013.

Carpenter, H. *The Inklings: C. S. Lewis, J. R. R. Tolkien, Charles Williams and their Friends*,.NSW: George Allen & Unwin, 1978.

Como, J. *Branches to Heaven: The Geniuses of C. S. Lewis*. Dallas: Spence, 1998.

_____. *Remembering C. S. Lewis*. San Francisco: Ignatius, 2006.

Connolly, S. *Inklings of Heaven: C. S. Lewis and Eschatology*. Leominster: Gracewing, 2007.

Downing, D. C. *Into the Region of Awe: Mysticism in C. S. Lewis*. Illinois: InterVarsity, 2005.

_____. *Planets in Peril: A Critical Study of C. S. Lewis's Ransom Trilogy*. Amherst: University of Massachusetts Press, 1992.

_____. *The Most Reluctant Convert: C .S. Lewis's Journey to Faith*. Illinois: InterVarsity, 2002.

Duriez, C., and D. Porter. *The Inklings Handbook: The Lives, Thought and Writings of C. S. Lewis, J. R. R. Tolkien, Charles Williams, Owen Barfield and their Friends*. Manchester: Chalice Press, 2001.

Duriez, C. *Tolkien and C. S. Lewis: The Gift of Friendship*. New Jersey: Paulist Press, 2003.

Lancelyn Green, R., and W. Hooper. *C. S. Lewis: A Biography*. London: HarperCollins, 2002.

Gresham, D. *Jack's Life: A Memory of C. S. Lewis*. Nashville: Broadman and Holman Publishers, 2005.

_____. *Lenten Lands: My Childhood with Joy Davidman and C. S. Lewis*. San Francisco: Harper, 1994.

Griffin, W. *C. S. Lewis: The Authentic Voice*. Wolverhampton: Lion, 2005.

Hooper, W. (ed.). *Collected Letters of C. S. Lewis, Vol. 1: Family Letters 1905–1931*. New York: HarperCollins, 2004.

_____(ed.). *Collected Letters of C. S. Lewis, Vol. 2: Books, Broadcasts and War 1931–1949*. New York: HarperCollins, 2004.

_____(ed.). *Collected Letters of C. S. Lewis, Vol. 3: Narnia, Cambridge and Joy 1950–1963*. New York: HarperCollins, 2007.

_____. *C. S. Lewis: A Companion and Guide*. London: HarperCollins, 1996.

_____(ed.). *They Stand Together: The Letters of C. S. Lewis to Arthur Greeves (1914–1963)*. London: HarperCollins, 1979.

_____. *Through Joy and Beyond: A Pictorial Biography of C. S. Lewis*. London: Macmillan, 1982.

Kennedy, J. *The Everything Guide to C. S. Lewis and Narnia*. London: Adams Media, 2008.

Kilby, C. S. *The Christian World of C. S. Lewis*. Michigan: Eerdmans, 1995.

Lowenberg, S. *C. S. Lewis: A Reference Guide 1972–1988*. Boston:

Hall & Co., 1993.

Martindale, W., and J. Root. *The Quotable Lewis*. Cambridge: Tyndale House Publishers, 1990.

McGrath, A. *C. S. Lewis – A Life: Eccentric Genius, Reluctant Prophet*. Illinois: Tyndale House Publishers, Inc., 2013.

Mills, D. (ed.). *The Pilgrim's Guide: C. S. Lewis and the Art of Witness*. Michigan: Eerdmans, 1998.

Pearce, J. *C. S. Lewis and the Catholic Church*. San Francisco: Ignatius Press, 2003.

Peters, T. C. *Simply C. S. Lewis: A Beginner's Guide to His Life and Works*. Derby: Kingsway Publications, 1998.

Phillips, J. *C. S. Lewis at the BBC: Messages of Hope in the Darkness of War*. London: Marshall Pickering, 2003.

Sayer, G. *Jack: C. S. Lewis and His Times*. London: Macmillan, 1988.

Wagner, R. J. *C. S. Lewis and Narnia for Dummies*. Hoboken: For Dummies, 2005.

Walsh, C. *C. S. Lewis: Apostle to the Skeptics*. London: Macmillan, 1949.

Ward, M. *Planet Narnia*. Oxford: Oxford University Press, 2008.

Wilson, A. N. *C. S. Lewis: A Biography*. New York: W.W. Norton, 1990.

Williams, B. M. *C. S. Lewis Pre-Evangelism for a Post- Christian World: Why Narnia Might Be More Real than We Think*. Cambridge, Ohio: Christian Publishing House, 2021.

Williams, R. *The Lion's World: A Journey into the Heart of Narnia*. Oxford: Oxford University Press, 2013.

About the Author

FINTAN MONAHAN is bishop of Killaloe, based in Ennis, Co. Clare, Ireland. This is the third book in his series on people whose lives and literary works have inspired him. The other books in the series are *A Perfect Peace: Newman, Saint for Our Time* (2019) and *Peace Smiles: Rediscovering Thomas Merton* (2020).